Summ

The 7 Habits of Highly Effective People

by Stephen R. Covey

Instaread

Please Note

This is a summary with analysis.

Table of Contents

Overview 5

Important People 7

Key Takeaways...8

Analysis 11

Key Takeaway 1 11

Key Takeaway 2 13

Key Takeaway 3 15

Key Takeaway 4 17

Key Takeaway 5 18

Key Takeaway 6 20

Key Takeaway 7 22

Key Takeaway 8 23

Key Takeaway 9 25

Key Takeaway 10 27

Key Takeaway 11 28

Author's Style 29

Author's Perspective 31

References 33

Overview

The 7 Habits of Highly Effective People is a self-help book that outlines seven skills to develop in order to increase efficiency and have more rewarding interpersonal relationships.

Living according to the seven habits requires paradigm shifts that allow an individual to become flexible enough to change. One is the shift in associations when considering independence and interdependence. Independence, which is more valued by contemporary personality-driven trends, can cause problematic isolation and stifle cooperation. Interdependence describes a healthier approach that enables teamwork. The seven habits also require an understanding of the difference between production, or results, and production capacity, the processes that generate the results, neither of which can be prioritized at the cost of the other.

The first three habits relate to private victories. First, people should restrict their efforts to the things that they can actually influence, and not waste energy on things that cause worry but cannot be directly controlled. Being proactive can expand the range of things that a person can influence. Second, the end goal should always be the focus. Leaders in particular are responsible for communicating desired focus, although they can be misled when they center their efforts elsewhere, such as on possessions or work. Third, fulfilling those goals requires careful self-management, which is best accomplished by focusing resources on things that are important, not just urgent.

The next three habits relate to public victories, which depend on the prerequisite private victories. First, the goal of any negotiation should be for both sides to consider the outcome a "win." Going into negotiations with the goal outcome being either win-win or no deal is the most beneficial to working relationships. Second, everyone should seek to understand before seeking to be understood, a principle achieved through empathic listening. Third, once the preceding habits are in place, people can practice synergy, wherein the variety of strengths in a team compensate for each member's weaknesses.

The final habit is to engage in constant self-renewal in the physical, spiritual, mental, and emotional or social dimensions. Doing so reinforces the other six habits.

The 7 Habits of Highly Effective People has sold more than 25 million copies in 40 languages since its initial publication in 1989. It is still one of the best-selling self-help books of all time, influencing business leaders worldwide as well as political leaders such as former US President Bill Clinton, who sought a personal consultation with Covey. The 2015 interactive edition includes updates and responses to frequently asked questions.

Important People

Stephen Covey (1932-2012) was a leadership consultant who wrote numerous books on the subject. He was a professor at Utah State University in the School of Business.

Sandra Covey was Stephen Covey's wife. Their relationship figures prominently in anecdotes that support arguments in *The 7 Habits of Highly Effective People.*

Viktor Frankl (1905-1997) was a psychiatrist who survived the Holocaust as a concentration camp prisoner. He founded a school of psychoanalysis called logotherapy, which sought to treat patients whose lives lacked meaning.

Muhammad Anwar El Sadat (1918-1981) was president of Egypt from 1970 to 1981, a time period that included the Yom Kippur War against Israel. Peace negotiations following the war earned him the Nobel Peace Prize.

Key Takeaways

1. To protect long-term productivity, assets that produce results should not be sacrificed for the sake of those results.

2. Individualism can create obstacles to teamwork. People who have achieved independence should still value interdependence.

3. The seven habits are all interrelated and mutually reinforcing. Some are associated with developing skills used to achieve private victories, and they reinforce the skills of other habits that lead to public victories.

4. Rather than waste energy on concerns outside their circles of influence, people should attempt to expand these circles through proactive work.

5. During the planning stages, people should focus on their end goals, which are informed by their driving philosophies and principles. Leaders need to embody such focus for their whole team.

6. Effective self-managers spend most of their time on the important things and know how to say no to things that are unimportant, even if they are urgent.

7. Relationships operate on a balance of give and take represented by an emotional bank account.

Deposits in the bank account include fulfilled commitments, while withdrawals involve failed commitments.

8. In negotiation, each party should attempt to reach a win-win resolution. The negotiation process is less damaging to the relationship when both parties can walk away from a resolution that represents a loss to either party.

9. Individuals should practice empathic listening, which focuses on seeing the situation from the other party's perspective, and seek to understand the other person before trying to be understood.

10. The first five habits enable a state of synergy among teams, where individuals work together with trust and cooperation and their various strengths benefit everyone. Synergistic teams find alternative win-win resolutions to problems.

11. The final habit is constant renewal of the different dimensions of skills, which enable more achievements of private and public victories.

Thank you for purchasing this Instaread book

**Download the Instaread mobile app to get
unlimited text & audio summaries
of bestselling books.**

Visit Instaread.co
to learn more.

Analysis

Key Takeaway 1

To protect long-term productivity, assets that produce results should not be sacrificed for the sake of those results.

Analysis

In the familiar fable, a farmer kills a goose that lays golden eggs in order to get more eggs immediately, only to discover that doing so prevents him from getting any more eggs. If production is valued above the assets that support production, production will suffer because production capacity was neglected.

Some companies take this principle to heart and give their employees a lot of power to control the means and manner of production, as Toyota famously does on its assembly lines. Workers are allowed to stop the production line at any time to fix a production error, a practice which other companies assumed would result in intoler-able delays and bankruptcy. Instead, Toyota's quality of output improved, and the employees used their power over the assembly line responsibly. [1] This demonstrates a way to protect just one of the three assets of production capacity, human assets; the other two being financial and physical assets. Preventive machine maintenance and soft-ware security updates are two activities that protect phys-ical assets. Responsible cash flow monitoring is a way to protect financial assets.

Key Takeaway 2

Individualism can create obstacles to teamwork. People who have achieved independence should still value interdependence.

Analysis

Over the past 50 years, self-help literature has focused on the personality ethic, which advocates self-esteem and individualism but gives people few tools for working interdependently. Prior to the personality ethic, the character ethic was more popular and promoted acting on principle. The personality ethic promotes independence, but strict independence can create obstacles to teamwork. In contrast, the character ethic supports healthy relationships and teamwork, which leads to rewarding interdependence through cooperation and community building.

The character ethic, with its support of interdependence, was a more popular approach to self-improvement in the late eighteenth century at the time of the American Revolution. The character ethic might be seen as the foundation for the cooperative model of the republic on which the US Constitution is based. The states ratified a shared set of principles drafted by delegates to the Constitutional Convention. When they did, they agreed to cooperate in order to uphold those principles. The idealistic cooperation of the individual states in the United States reflects the value of interdependence, since the states are not entirely dependent on each other and they reinforce each other with a variety of strengths. Not every state has a major financial center, and those states without one might produce more in agriculture.

Key Takeaway 3

The seven habits are all interrelated and mutually reinforcing. Some are associated with developing skills used to achieve private victories, and they reinforce the skills of other habits that lead to public victories.

Analysis

The three private habits state that people should be proactive within a circle of influence, imagine the end goals when making plans, and manage use of time to ensure important things get finished. Those habits do not involve interpersonal relationships. Habits four, five, and six, by contrast, involve others. They state that people should seek win-win solutions, attempt to understand others first, and reinforce synergy. People with few private skills will find the public skills much more difficult, so private victories are the first step toward public victories.

For example, a man who wants to use the seven habits to become a better department manager might wish to start by reforming the company's team structures, beginning with the ways that employees report to him. He could decide to remove competitive rewards in his department and replace them with systems that reward cooperation among his employees. However, he would find that difficult to achieve if he has yet to learn to devote more time to the important things on his to-do list, such as regular check-in meetings with his employees and with other division heads, rather than things that are more urgent but less important, such as attending an upcoming motivation seminar that would require him to postpone those meetings. Similarly, any public initiatives to motivate employees would be undermined if he devoted his efforts to tasks outside his sphere of influence, such as by trying to alter the activities of employees in other departments to benefit his own. The interpersonal habits might be more appealing than the first three private habits because they offer benefits across the entire team, but the private habits make the public habits more achievable.

Key Takeaway 4

Rather than waste energy on concerns outside their circles of influence, people should attempt to expand these circles through proactive work.

Analysis

For most people, their circles of concern are much larger than the circles of things they can actually influence. That circle of influence can expand if people are proactive, such as when an employee anticipates and resolves a boss's needs and is then given more responsibility.

The simplest example of people's activities expanding their circle of influence is when productivity results in a promotion. Proactive employees complete more tasks than their colleagues, so they would be natural candidates for promotion to management positions, where they could propose new ways for the employees to work and increase their productivity. Before the promotion, that employee would have little influence over coworkers and how they are motivated because the manager's initiatives would take priority. On the other hand, if an employee were promoted to a management position, he or she would still have little influence over how executives do their jobs and motivate the other managers.

Key Takeaway 5

During the planning stages, people should focus on their end goals, which are informed by their driving philosophies and principles. Leaders need to embody such focus for their whole team.

Analysis

Every task goes through two creation phases. The first is the planning phase and the second is the implementation. Both phases require consistent focus by leadership. Planning with the end result in mind prevents expensive course corrections, and it is the leader's responsibility to have that goal in mind to ensure everyone's efforts are still on the right course. The focus of the leader's vision changes depending on whether he or she focuses on principles or on other areas, such as family or money. Effective planning requires participation from both sides of the brain, broadening perspective of the issues involved, visualization of the goal, and principled affirmations.

One scenario in which this habit would be particularly important would be when a nonprofit plans an event to raise awareness of a cause, such as a disease. The nonprofit's stated focus is raising money for research into potential cures for the disease and supporting the families affected by it. The event would be intended to support that focus by connecting with influential community members and seeking donations from them, but from there, the focus on the fundraising and networking goals could shift as planning progresses. A planner might decide that the event should be a lavish gala to attract the community influencers, and a large amount of the event's budget would be spent on decoration, food, waitstaff, and paying for appearances by celebrity personalities. If leaders lose sight of the organization's principles and instead focus on popularity and status, the resulting implementation of the plan, the event itself, could cost the organization more money than it raised for research and fail to attract influential people who are genuinely interested in supporting its cause. If this were to occur, then the group would have been better off writing researchers a check for the cost of the event. A leader with a focus on the organization's principles would rein in spending and find ways to keep the event's focus on the individuals affected by the disease.

Key Takeaway 6

Effective self-managers spend most of their time on the important things and know how to say no to things that are unimportant, even if they are urgent.

Analysis

There are four types of activities, divided into categories of either urgent or not urgent and important or not important. People tend to devote too little time to important, non-urgent tasks at work and too much time to urgent, unimportant tasks. The most effective planning strategy is to lay out a schedule for the week in advance, allowing flexibility for each day.

For a woman who is a software company executive, urgent and important work would appear frequently because divisions of the company must push security updates to users and fix glitches in the products. A focus on important but not yet urgent tasks would facilitate some of her important work, such as creating programs for code security reviews or mandating more time for the program to be tested in quality assurance. But instead of this important work, the executive might have spent her time in urgent but unimportant tasks, such as market research to decide which products should be developed next. That task is less important than preserving the company's reputation for quality products, since a new product released by an unreliable company would not sell as well as a product from a company with a better reputation, even if it were released later. The executive should also not spend much time on tasks that are neither important nor urgent, such as writing blog posts on a personal platform, when more important tasks are pressing. In the future, the increased code security reviews and quality assurance testing would decrease the time spent on urgent and important work, and the executive could spend time on market research while also having more time to spend on important but not urgent work, such as improving employee engagement.

Key Takeaway 7

Relationships operate on a balance of give and take represented by an emotional bank account. Deposits in the bank account include fulfilled commitments, while withdrawals involve failed commitments.

Analysis

Customer relationships can be some of the most influential in a company's success or failure. A company with a reputation for having unbalanced emotional bank accounts with customers will find it difficult to regain their trust. Two companies that saw some of the most embarrassing customer relationship incidents in 2015, Time Warner Cable and Comcast, saw their scores on the American Consumer Satisfaction Index continue to fall even though they were already toward the bottom of the rankings. Cable companies were also the lowest-ranked category in the entire index. [2] These negative reputations are due to constant withdrawals from their emotional bank accounts with their customers, through pushy sales tactics, failure to meet commitments, and complete lack of deposits in those accounts by failing to provide reliable cable and internet service. In order to bring those accounts back into balance, the companies would need to demonstrate that they understand their customers' values, clarify their expectations for themselves and their customers, fulfill commitments, and make sincere apologies when they withdraw from their emotional bank accounts.

Key Takeaway 8

In negotiation, each party should attempt to reach a win-win resolution. The negotiation process is less damaging to the relationship when both parties can walk away from a resolution that represents a loss to either party.

Analysis

The best approach to negotiation is for both parties to begin with the understanding that they will not be expected to accept a resolution that would be a loss for them. These negotiations require character traits such as integrity, maturity, and a belief that abundant resources exist for all parties to be satisfied.

One of the strategies recommended by the authors of *Getting to Yes*, a classic text on negotiation, is for each party to know their best alternative to a negotiated resolution. This represents an advantage for the negotiating parties, because they know ahead of time how good a resolution would need to be in order to be preferable to the "no deal" alternative. [3] For two companies negotiating changes to a software vendor contract, the customer might already know which vendor they will choose if they cannot get a contract that guarantees software solutions more closely customized for their needs. The price for the alternative vendor might be higher and the time needed to switch systems would be costly, but still preferable to not having needed features. On the other hand, the vendor might be afraid of losing its largest customer and need to weigh the cost of losing the contract against the cost of changing the software and developing new features. A win-win solution might include a higher price for the contract to compensate for the vendor's expense of developing the new features, but would keep the vendor profitable and save the customer the hassle and expense of switching systems.

Key Takeaway 9

Individuals should practice empathic listening, which focuses on seeing the situation from the other party's perspective, and seek to understand the other person before trying to be understood.

Analysis

Some people listen only with the goal of forming a response or making some connection to their own life. Empathic listening involves completely removing these distracting motivations and focusing on understanding the other person, in order to avoid providing inappropriate advice and to earn trust through the conversation.

Psychologists' understanding of empathy is evolving with the study of individuals who have autism spectrum disorders. People with autism are generally believed to lack the ability to understand what others are thinking or feeling based on facial expressions and social cues. Empathic conversation would require the ability to see beyond the content of the conversation and observe all of the other factors that demonstrate emotion; people with autism spectrum disorders struggle with these cues. However, those people might not be entirely without empathy, since recent research indicates that they can make decisions based on pro-social morals, or morals that benefit others as much as themselves. [4] Individuals attempting to cultivate the seventh habit could apply the concept of pro-social morals to develop a pro-social habit of conversation, wherein the goal is to ensure they are adjusting their responses and body language according to their understanding of their interlocutor's emotional state.

Key Takeaway 10

The first five habits enable a state of synergy among teams, where individuals work together with trust and cooperation and their various strengths benefit everyone. Synergistic teams find alternative win-win resolutions to problems.

Analysis

Synergy is a state of teamwork where many people are providing input, which requires trust and cooperation. A team that is working in a state of synergy can identify win-win alternative solutions and move the status quo.

A synergistic team looks more like a panel discussion with a minimally intrusive moderator than it does like a classroom or seminar, a comparison which demonstrates that the size of the group matters when promoting synergy. A panel discussion is smaller because interactivity is difficult to coordinate across dozens of people. When a large group meets to make decisions, the likelihood that everyone will participate is lower. Teams with low synergy might try breaking the team into smaller subgroups to promote stronger familiarity and trust.

Key Takeaway 11

The final habit is constant renewal of the different dimensions of skills, which enable more achievements of private and public victories.

Analysis

The habit of balanced self-renewal through physical, spiritual, mental, and social or emotional dimensions can increase physical energy, reinforce the values systems that support principled action, broaden perspective to improve decision-making, and strengthen relationships with frequent collaborators.

For example, a manager who has already incorporated the other six habits into his life can begin practicing the seventh habit by achieving a physical, spiritual, or mental victory every day and building up the emotional bank account for people with whom he works often. On any given day, he might work out for a half-hour to increase his stamina during the work week, read about compassion or ethics to reinforce his commitment to his principles, or watch a lecture on a technical topic in his field of work to help him make informed decisions. Then, he could build on his social and emotional skills by learning about his employees' values, fulfilling a commitment to his boss, or doing some small kindness for his fellow managers.

Author's Style

Stephen Covey writes in a style that ranges from casual to formal. Much of the book contains formal or high diction, but Covey relates anecdotes from his personal and business life in a conversational style with dialogue driving those encounters. Covey's prevailing style is lecture-like, and he often addresses the reader. The way he communicates hypotheticals and refers to the reader in them changes throughout the book. Early in the book, all hypotheticals are described as if they were happening to Covey. Later he addresses the reader as "you" and describes hypothetical happenings to "us."

Most of the examples and anecdotes Covey cites come from his personal life. A slightly smaller amount of space is allocated to cases on which Covey consulted, business decisions he made, and classes he taught. Covey cites a handful of recent historical examples, told in broad overview. He also quotes spiritual sources, historical figures, and allegories.

Covey's consulting clients and the businesses for which they worked are not named when he describes their cases. In some of the private-life anecdotes, which of Covey's children was involved in certain incidents is not specified. In others, Covey states which child was involved and sometimes describes personal details, such as illness symptoms.

Although *The 7 Habits of Highly Effective People* is a self-help book with a consistent focus on business, most chapters have a heavy emphasis on parenting. Covey pulls extensively from his experience raising his children and managing his marriage. Many examples in the book deliver lessons on balancing work and family, convincing children to do chores, and opening up lines of communication between spouses.

Covey's language is not technical, and there are no instances in which Covey dives deep enough into a particular business to necessitate describing any technical topics.

Most chapters include one or more infographics, which incorporate text from elsewhere in the chapter with visual reinforcement and artistically arranged text. There is no consistent chapter structure throughout the book.

Author's Perspective

Stephen Covey earned his master's degree in business administration from Harvard University, followed by a doctoral degree in religious education from Brigham Young University. *The 7 Habits of Highly Effective People* was his first book that focused on leadership education rather than religion. He continued to write about leadership. Covey received many awards for his work in leadership teaching. He was named to *Time* magazine's 1996 list of the 25 most influential Americans. He taught at Utah State University's Jon Huntsman School of Business and established the company that would eventually become FranklinCovey, a leadership and productivity training firm.

~~~~ END OF INSTAREAD ~~~~

Thank you for purchasing this Instaread book

**Download the Instaread mobile app to get
unlimited text & audio summaries
of bestselling books.**

Visit Instaread.co
to learn more.

References

1. Duhigg, Charles. *Smarter Better Faster*. New York: Random House, 2016.

2. Kline, Daniel. "Comcast, Time Warner Cable Still Rank Worst In Customer Service." *The Motley Fool*. June 3, 2015. Accessed March 30, 2016. http://www.fool.com/investing/general/2015/06/03/comcast-time-warner-cable-still-rank-worst-in-cust.aspx

3. Fisher, Roger, and William Ury. *Getting to Yes: Negotiating Agreement Without Giving In*. London: Penguin Books 2012.

4. Gregoire, Carolyn. "We May Have Been Wrong About Autism And Empathy." *Huffington Post*. March 29, 2016. Accessed March 30, 2016. http://www.huffingtonpost.com/entry/autism-empathy-brain-research_us_56f92575e4b014d3fe237413

Lightning Source UK Ltd.
Milton Keynes UK
UKOW06f1904220617
303924UK00013B/323/P